Heinemann First
ENCYCLOPEDIA

Volume 3
Chr-Dru

Heinemann Library
Chicago, Illinois

Series Editors: Rebecca and Stephen Vickers, Gianna Williams
Author Team: Rob Alcraft, Catherine Chambers, Sabrina Crewe, Jim Drake, Fred Martin, Angela Royston, Jane Shuter, Roger Thomas, Rebecca Vickers, Stephen Vickers

This revised and expanded edition produced for Heinemann Library by Discovery Books.
Photo research by Katherine Smith and Rachel Tisdale
Designed by Keith Williams, Michelle Lisseter, and Gecko
Illustrations by Stefan Chabluk and Mark Bergin

Originated by Ambassador Litho Limited
Printed in China by WKT Company Limited

10 09 08 07 06
10 9 8 7 6 5 4 3 2

Library of Congress Cataloging-in-Publication Data

Heinemann first encyclopedia.
    p.   cm.
    Summary: A fourteen-volume encyclopedia covering animals, plants, countries, transportation, science, ancient civilizations, US states, US presidents, and world history
    ISBN 1-4034-7110-X (v. 3 : lib. bdg.)
    1. Children's encyclopedias and dictionaries.
I. Heinemann Library (Firm)
AG5.H45 2005
031—dc22   2005006176

Acknowledgments
Cover: Cover photographs of a desert, an electric guitar, a speedboat, an iceberg, a man on a camel, cactus flowers, and the Colosseum at night reproduced with permission of Corbis. Cover photograph of the Taj Mahal reproduced with permission of Digital Stock. Cover photograph of an x-ray of a man, and the penguins reproduced with permission of Digital Vision. Cover photographs of a giraffe, the Leaning Tower of Pisa, the Statue of Liberty, a white owl, a cactus, a butterfly, a saxophone, an astronaut, cars at night, and a circuit board reproduced with permission of Getty Images/Photodisc. Cover photograph of Raglan Castle reproduced with permission of Peter Evans; Clive Barda, p. 6; J. Allan Cash Ltd., pp. 13 bottom, 23, 27, 32, 40; Ardea London Ltd, p. 44 top; Kate Atkinson, p. 10 bottom; Bob Bennett, p. 24 bottom; G.I. Bernard, p. 10 top; Bruce Coleman/Jane Burton, p. 30; Des Conway, p. 33 top; John Cooke, p. 25 bottom; Daniel J. Cox, pp. 24 top, 36 top; Steve Dunwell/The Image Bank, p. 19; Don Emmert/AFP/Getty Images, p. 8 bottom; Sarah Errington, p. 39; FLPA/Marineland, p. 44 bottom; GSF Picture Library, p. 42; Getty Images/PhotoDisk, p. 14; Mark Hamblin, p. 9 bottom; Jeremy A. Horner, p. 11; Hulton Archive/Getty Images, p. 35 bottom; The Hutchison Library, p. 4; Image Bank/Gary Gladstone, p. 17 top; Tim Jackson, p. 34; Kobal Collection/Merrick Morton, p. 47 bottom; Jeffrey Lang, p. 28 bottom; C.C. Lockwood, p. 38 top; Jerry Lodriguss, p. 16 top; MPI/Getty Images, p. 15 top; John McCammon, p. 29 top; Medimage/Antony King, p. 18; Margaret Miller, p. 43 bottom; Oxford Scientific Films, p. 46; Performing Arts Library/Colin Willoughbey, p. 47 top; Peter Parks, p. 22; Pekka Parvianen, p. 16 top; Robert Pearcy, p. 43 bottom; Christine Pemberton, p. 31; Jake Rajs/Stone, p. 37; Redferns/Simon King, p. 33 bottom; B. Regent, p. 45; Rex Features, p.48 top; Royal Geographical Society, p. 9 top; Leonard Lee Rue III, p. 36 bottom; Kjell Sandved, p. 25 top; Science Photo Library, p. 38 bottom; Hugh Sitton, p. 41; Jake Rajs/Stone, p. 37; Justin Sullivan/Getty Images, p. 8 top; Three Lions/Getty Images, p. 15; John Tilford, p. 26 top; Geoff Tompkinson, p. 48 bottom; Tom Ulrich, pp. 28 top, 29 bottom; Fred Whitehead, p. 26 bottom; Library of Congress, p. 15 bottom.

Welcome to
Heinemann First Encyclopedia

What is an encyclopedia?

An encyclopedia is an information book. It gives the most important facts about many different subjects. This encyclopedia has been written for children who are using an encyclopedia for the first time. It covers many of the subjects from school and others you may find interesting.

What is in this encyclopedia?

In this encyclopedia, each topic is called an *entry*. There is one page of information for every entry. The entries in this encyclopedia explain

- animals
- plants
- dinosaurs
- countries
- geography
- history
- world religions
- music
- art
- transportation
- science
- technology
- states
- famous Americans

How to use this encyclopedia

This encyclopedia has thirteen books called *volumes*. The first twelve volumes contain entries. The entries are all in alphabetical order. This means that Volume 1 starts with entries that begin with the letter A and Volume 12 ends with entries that begin with the letter Z. Volume 13 is the index volume. It also has other interesting information.

Here are two entries that show you what you can find on a page:

The "see also" line tells you where to find other related information.

This is the letter that the entry starts with.

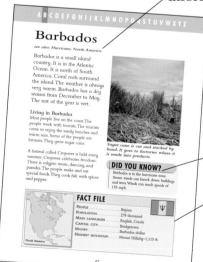

Fact boxes give you details about the topic.

Did You Know? *boxes have fun or interesting bits of information.*

The Fact File tells you important facts and figures.

Christianity

see also: Cathedral, Israel

Christianity is a world religion. Its followers are called Christians. The religion comes from the teachings of Jesus Christ. Christians believe that Jesus is the son of God.

The life of Jesus Christ

Jesus was born about 2,000 years ago in Palestine. He was a carpenter. He became a famous preacher. People traveled far to hear him talk. Jesus talked about how people could change their lives. Government and other religious leaders were worried. They did not want the people to follow Jesus. Jesus was put to death.

This is a Christian service in South Africa.

Beliefs and teachings

The followers of Jesus believe that he rose up from the dead. They began teaching what Jesus taught. This was the beginnings of Christianity. The New Testament in the Bible tells the story. It tells of Jesus and his teachings.

Christianity today

There are about 2 billion Christians in the world. Christians worship at home and in churches. The most important Christian festival is Easter. Easter celebrates Jesus' death and rebirth.

This modern Christian church in California is called the Crystal Cathedral.

Civil War

see also: Lincoln, Abraham; Slavery

A civil war is a war between people of the same country. A civil war happens when people in a nation become divided. The United States fought a civil war from 1861 to 1865.

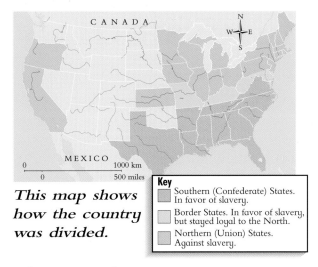

This map shows how the country was divided.

Key
- Southern (Confederate) States. In favor of slavery.
- Border States. In favor of slavery, but stayed loyal to the North.
- Northern (Union) States. Against slavery.

North and south

In the 1800s, the people of the United States of America became divided. One of the reasons northern states fought with southern states was slavery. Many people in southern states kept slaves. Slaves worked on large plantations. People in the North believed slavery was wrong.

The Confederate states

In 1860, Americans elected Abraham Lincoln as president. Lincoln was against slavery. People in the southern states did not want him as their president. The southern states decided to form their own nation. It was called the Confederate States of America.

The war

President Lincoln said the United States could not be divided. The Civil War began. The South was fighting for the right to make its own rules and laws. The North was fighting to keep the nation together and to end slavery. Many thousands of people were killed and wounded. Farms and houses were destroyed.

The northern army had more soldiers, weapons, and supplies. After four years of fighting, the southern army was losing. The Confederate commander was General Robert E. Lee. In 1865, he decided to surrender. The Civil War ended. The United States was reunited.

More than 600,000 soldiers died in the Civil War.

Classical Music

see also: Music, Musical Instrument

Classical music is written for groups of instruments, such as orchestras. Classical music is also written for singers. People who write music are called composers.

The first classical music

At first, music was played by one instrument. Sometimes people sang or chanted music in churches. Then classical music began in the 1500s in Europe. Composers wrote classical music. They wrote for bigger groups of instruments.

Rulers and nobles paid to have music written and performed. People started music colleges. The colleges taught classical music. Concerts of classical music were performed for the people. Anyone could go to a concert.

TYPES OF CLASSICAL MUSIC

Symphony	A long piece of music written for a group of musicians in an orchestra.
Concerto	A piece of music written for an orchestra. One instrument plays the most important part.
Chamber music	Music written for a small orchestra or small group of instruments.
Opera	A play set to music. It has an orchestra and a chorus of singers. Singers called soloists act and sing the important parts.
Choral music	Music for a group of singers. There may also be an orchestra or instruments playing with them.

JOHANN SEBASTIAN BACH (1685–1750)

Bach was a famous composer from Germany. His family played music. He played the violin and the viola. He wrote music for groups of instruments. He wrote music for the organ. He wrote music for singers.

This small orchestra plays classical music.

Climate

see also: Season, Weather

Climate is the pattern of heat, wind, and rain in a region. The day-to-day change of heat, wind, and rain is called weather.

Climate and seasons

Most places in the world have a pattern of weather. This pattern breaks the year into parts. The parts are called seasons. The types of seasons tell the kind of climate.

Six climate regions

1. **Polar regions** – These areas are very cold all year round.

2. **Cold regions** – These areas have a short spring and a short summer. It never gets very warm.

3. **Cold temperate regions** – These areas have four different seasons. Winter is very cold. Summer is warm.

4. **Warm temperate regions** – These areas have four seasons. Summer is very hot. Winter does not get very cold.

5. **Dry regions** – There is little or no rain. All deserts are dry regions.

6. **Tropical regions** – These areas have heavy rain all year. There are swamps and rain forests.

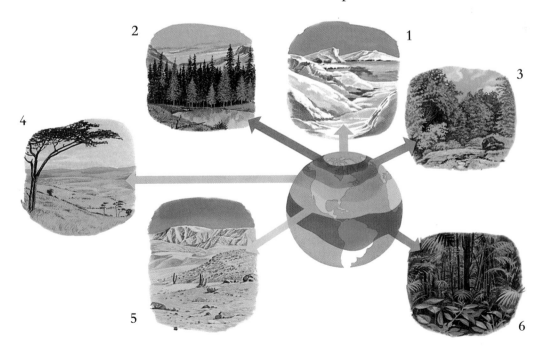

Clinton, Bill

Bill Clinton was the 42nd president of the United States of America.

Clinton enters politics

Clinton went to high school in Hot Springs, Arkansas. He met President Kennedy on a school trip to Washington, D.C. He became interested in politics.

Clinton trained to be a lawyer. In 1975, he married Hillary Rodham. After teaching law, Clinton became a politician. He served as attorney general and governor for the state of Arkansas.

DID YOU KNOW?

Clinton was impeached while he was president. That means he went on trial before Congress. Clinton was accused of lying. He was found not guilty.

Crowds on Capitol Hill watch Clinton being sworn in as president.

Clinton becomes president

Clinton was elected president in 1993. The United States was prosperous during Clinton's presidency. This made Clinton popular. Clinton was also popular in other countries. He involved the United States in peace-keeping missions abroad.

Bill Clinton was a Democrat.

FACT FILE

DATE OF BIRTH	August 19, 1946
BIRTHPLACE	Hope, Arkansas
PRESIDENTIAL NUMBER	42
DATES IN OFFICE	1993–2001
POLITICAL PARTY	Democrat
VICE PRESIDENT	Al Gore
FIRST LADY	Hillary Rodham Clinton

Coast

see also: Bay, Delta

The coast is where land meets the sea. The edge of the land is called the coastline. Some coasts have steep cliffs. This is where mountains come down into the sea. Other coasts have wide beaches. Coastlines may have bays or rivers running into the sea.

How coasts change

The coastline is always changing. Waves wear away some parts of a coast. Waves splash against rock along the coast. After thousands of years, some of the rock is broken up. It is broken into tiny pieces. It is washed up on the land. This becomes a beach.

The waves of the sea are wearing away this coastline. This is called erosion. Buildings near the edge are unsafe. They may fall off the edge into the sea.

People and the coast

Sometimes the sea is rough. It washes away the coastline. Roads and houses may be washed away. People build concrete and stone walls to protect the coast. Tourists and people who live along the sea enjoy the coasts. They swim and sail. Some people make a living by fishing. There are large harbors along the coast. This is where ships come to load and unload goods.

This coast is partly high chalk cliffs. The cliffs go into the sea. This is also a rocky coast.

Cockroach

see also: Insect

A cockroach is an insect. Most cockroaches live outdoors. They live in hot, tropical countries. They also live in houses. The cockroach is a household pest.

Cockroach families

The female cockroach lays eggs in a tough egg case. The eggs hatch into nymphs. A nymph looks like an adult, but it has no wings. Cockroaches hide in houses. They hide in walls, cupboards, and small spaces. They hide outside under stones, and in logs, bark, and ant nests.

COCKROACH FACTS

NUMBER OF DIFFERENT KINDS...	3,500
COLOR	usually black or brown
LENGTH	up to 4 inches
STATUS	common
LIFE SPAN...........	about 2 years
ENEMIES	spiders, birds, people

thick, leathery skin for protection

long antennae to smell food

an American cockroach

hairs on its legs to touch and feel things

PLANT, INSECT, AND MEAT EATER

The cockroach eats at night. It eats any food and drinks any water it can find. Dirty plates, pet food, and spilled food attract cockroaches.

This is a female giant burrowing cockroach with her nymphs. Cockroaches live everywhere. They spread to new places in airplanes, ships, and trains.

Colombia

see also: South America

Colombia is a country in South America. The Andes Mountains run from north to south in Colombia. In the east are grassy, flat lands and hot, wet jungle.

Living in Columbia

Most Colombians live in cities. The cities are crowded with buses and cars. People sell candy and fruit on the street. There are big farms in the country. People grow coffee and sugar. Many farmers have very little land. It is hard for them to make enough money to live.

Colombians grow and eat a lot of corn. They use the corn to make soups, stews, and drinks. They make tortillas from corn flour.

DID YOU KNOW?

Most of the emeralds used in jewelry come from Colombia.

One of Colombia's largest crops is coffee. Coffee beans are picked from coffee bushes.

South America

FACT FILE

PEOPLE	Colombians
POPULATION	about 42 million
MAIN LANGUAGE	Spanish
CAPITAL CITY	Bogotá
MONEY	Colombian peso
HIGHEST MOUNTAIN	Pico Cristóbal Colón–18,947 feet
LONGEST RIVER	Magdalena River–993 miles

Colonial America

see also: American Revolution;
Columbus, Christopher

Colonial America was when European settlers founded colonies in North America. A colony is a place where people come and settle. A colony is often ruled by another country.

Europeans arrive

After Christopher Columbus sailed to the American continent in 1492, European settlers founded colonies there. France, Britain, and Spain all claimed large areas of North America.

The thirteen colonies

The first English colony was Jamestown, Virginia. It was settled in 1607. By 1733 there were thirteen English colonies.

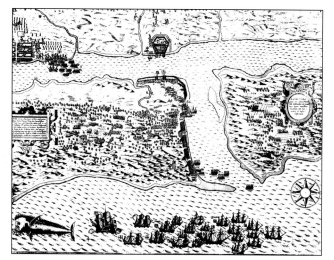

The Spanish colony of St. Augustine, Florida, was one of the first European colonies.

KEY DATES

1492	Christopher Columbus makes his first voyage to America.
1607	First colony at Jamestown, Virginia is founded.
1733	There are 13 British colonies.
1775	Colonists fight first battles against British troops.

In 1773 angry colonists dumped British tea into Boston Harbor. This is called the Boston Tea Party.

The people there built towns, farms, and churches. The colonists' lives were often hard, but they were proud to have their own land. They struggled to survive. With the colonists' hard work, the colonies grew larger and produced many goods.

Britain ruled the colonies. Often the laws and taxes that Britain made were unpopular with the colonists. In 1775 the colonists decided to fight Britain. The American Revolution had begun.

Color

see also: Light

Color is seen when light bounces off an object. The light bounces into the eyes of the person looking at the color. The color we see is the light that has bounced into our eyes.

Different colors

There are three primary, or main, colors when we use paint or ink. The colors are red, blue, and yellow. Any other color can be made by mixing these colors. All the colors mixed together make an almost black color.

The three primary colors when we use colored light are red, blue, and green. Any colored light can be made by mixing these lights. All the light colors mixed together make white light.

Using color

The pictures on color TV are made of tiny dots. These dots are red, blue, and green light. Color can be used in signals. Color is used in flags and traffic lights. Color can be used as a danger signal.

Animals use color. Color helps them find a mate, scare away enemies, and helps them hide.

DID YOU KNOW?

Black and white are not real colors. When all the light bounces back, an object looks white. When no light bounces back, an object looks black.

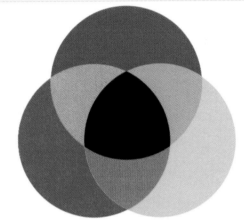

Colors of paint and ink can be mixed to make different colors.

The red, yellow, and green colors used in traffic lights are well-known signals.

Colorado

see also: United States of America

Colorado is a state in the western United States of America. It is the highest state in the nation. There are many mountains there. There are hills and areas of high plains, too. Colorado gets lots of snow and sunshine.

In the past
Long ago, the Ancestral Puebloan people of the Southwest lived in Colorado. At a place called Mesa Verde, the Ancestral Puebloan built their homes in the sides of steep cliffs. Some of the houses are still there.

Life in Colorado
In Colorado ranchers raise cattle. Farmers grow corn, hay, and wheat. Many people who live in Colorado work in factories making computers and machinery. Other people in the state work for the government.

Cliff Palace in Mesa Verde National Park was built by Ancestral Puebloan Native Americans.

DID YOU KNOW?
The United States celebrated its centennial in 1876. It had been a nation for one hundred years. Colorado became a state the same year. That is why it is called the "Centennial State."

The United States Mint in Denver makes coins and stores gold and silver for the whole nation. People visit Colorado to ski and hike in the Rocky Mountains.

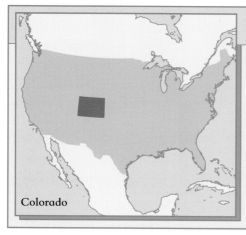

Colorado

FACT FILE

BECAME A STATE	1876 (38th state)
LAND AREA	103,718 square miles (8th largest land area)
POPULATION	4,550,688 (22nd most populated state)
OTHER NAME	Centennial State
CAPITAL CITY	Denver

Columbus, Christopher

see also: Bahamas, Colonial America, Cuba, Venezuela

Christopher Columbus was an explorer. He sailed to the continent of America.

Columbus the sailor

Columbus was born in Genoa, Italy. When he was about fourteen, Columbus became a sailor. He sailed along the Atlantic coast of Africa. Columbus wanted to sail west from Europe to Asia. Many people thought the earth was flat and that a ship might fall off the edge.

The voyages

In 1492, the king and queen of Spain gave Columbus money and ships. On October 12, 1492, Columbus's expedition landed on an island in the Bahamas. Columbus named it San Salvador. He named the people there Indians because he thought he was near India.

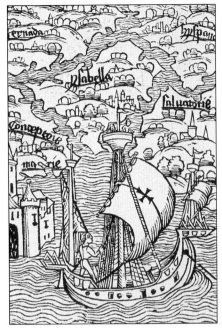

This drawing of Columbus was made during his lifetime.

Columbus made three more journeys to the Americas. He took Spanish people to found settlements in the Caribbean.

KEY DATES

1451 .. Christopher Columbus is born.
1492 .. Columbus makes first voyage to the Americas.
1493 .. Columbus makes second voyage.
1498 .. Columbus makes third voyage.
1502 .. Columbus makes fourth voyage.
1506 .. Columbus dies.

Christopher Columbus

Comet

see also: Solar System

A comet is a giant ball of ice, dust, gases, and rock. A comet moves through space. It looks like a star with a glowing tail. Comets are only seen when they get close to the sun.

What makes a comet?

There are many comets in the solar system. Most are far from the sun. They are frozen in cold outer space. The comet becomes hotter when it is pulled closer to the sun. It begins to boil away. This makes the comet's long tail. Most comets can only be seen with a telescope. A very bright comet can be seen in the night sky.

Halley's comet will next be seen in the year 2062.

A comet's journey

Some comets travel around the sun. The path they take is called an orbit. It takes the comet the same number of years for each orbit around the sun.

DID YOU KNOW?

Halley's Comet is seen from the earth every 76 years. It is named after the English astronomer Edmond Halley. He first saw the comet in 1682. He figured out when people could see it next.

This is the Hale-Bopp comet. It could be seen from Earth in 1997. The blue tail is made of gases. The white tail is dust. The gases and dust come from the comet head.

Communication

see also: Computer, Internet, Radio, Telephone, Television

Communication means sending messages. Messages can be information, ideas, or feelings. Speaking, writing, and the expression on a person's face are all communication.

Changes in communication

Letters were once the only way to send messages. The telegraph was first used in 1844. The telegraph sent electric messages along wires. The messages were in Morse code. Alexander Graham Bell invented the telephone in 1876. Today fax and e-mail messages are sent along telephone wires.

Radio and TV changed communication. Radio was invented in 1895. Radio signals move through the air. They do not need wires. Television uses radio signals to send moving pictures.

Light can carry messages. The messages move along wires. The wires are called optical fibers. Thousands of messages go along each fiber. Cable-TV uses optical cables.

This communications center uses telephones and computers.

Satellites circle the earth in space. They bounce signals such as telephone calls. The signals bounce from one side of the earth to the other side.

Computer

see also: Bar Code, Laser

A computer is a machine. It handles information quickly. Computers control many things. Computers control cars and even washing machines.

The first computers

Charles Babbage built the first computer. It was invented in England in 1833. ENIAC was the first electronic computer. It was built in the United States in 1946. It was the size of a small house.

Smaller and better

Electronics got better. The tiny microchip was made in the 1960s. It does the job of a large computer. Computers became smaller and more powerful.

The first personal computers were made around 1975. They were desktop computers made for people to use at home. They were about as powerful as the huge ENIAC. Today computers are even smaller. They get faster and more powerful all the time.

a personal computer

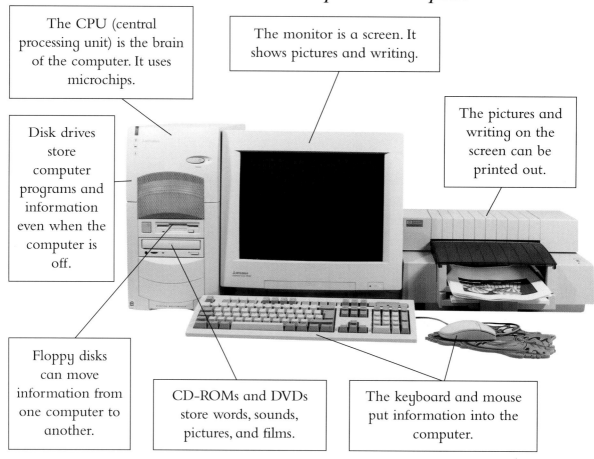

The CPU (central processing unit) is the brain of the computer. It uses microchips.

The monitor is a screen. It shows pictures and writing.

The pictures and writing on the screen can be printed out.

Disk drives store computer programs and information even when the computer is off.

Floppy disks can move information from one computer to another.

CD-ROMs and DVDs store words, sounds, pictures, and films.

The keyboard and mouse put information into the computer.

Connecticut

see also: United States of America

Connecticut is a state in the northeastern United States of America. It is in New England. The state has many hills, lakes, and streams. There are beaches in the southern part of the state. The summers in Connecticut are warm. It often snows there in winter.

Hartford, the capital of Connecticut, has many modern buildings.

Life in Connecticut

Connecticut is not very big, but many people live there. Most people live in cities and suburbs. Hartford is one of the three biggest cities in the state. Many people work in offices in Hartford. New Haven is another big city. Yale University is in New Haven. It is one of the most famous universities in the United States.

Connecticut has many factories. People in the factories make weapons, engines, tools, and submarines.

In the summer, people visit Connecticut's lakes and beaches. The beaches run along Long Island Sound. People swim, fish, and sail boats in Long Island Sound.

DID YOU KNOW?

Connecticut is the only state with a state hero. He is Nathan Hale, a teacher who became a spy. He spied for George Washington against the British in the American Revolution.

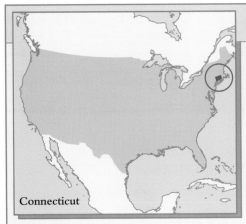

Connecticut

FACT FILE

BECAME A STATE... 1788 (5th state)

LAND AREA......... 4,845 square miles
(48th largest land area)

POPULATION 3,483,372
(29th most populated state)

OTHER NAMES ..... Constitution State, Nutmeg State

CAPITAL CITY ...... Hartford

Constitution

see also: Executive Branch, Government, Judicial Branch, Legislative Branch

A constitution is a set of rules for governing a nation. The United States Constitution says how the United States of America should be governed and what its main laws are.

The Preamble, at the beginning of the Constitution, explains why the Constitution was written.

Creating the Constitution

In 1783, the United States had won independence from Britain. Now the people needed to decide what kind of government they wanted. A big meeting took place in Philadelphia. It was the Constitutional Convention. Delegates from all over the United States talked and argued for months. Then in 1787 they approved and signed the Constitution.

KEY DATES

1774	First Continental Congress meets.
1783	American Revolution officially ends with the Treaty of Paris.
1787	Constitution is signed by delegates at the Constitutional Convention.
1789	Constitution goes into effect.
1791	Bill of Rights is added to the Constitution.

Government powers

The Constitution says the U.S. government was created by the people. It lays out the powers of different branches of government. It says how power should be divided between state governments and the U.S. government, or federal government.

Amendments and the Bill of Rights

The creators of the Constitution knew that it might need to be changed later. They said amendments, or changes, could be added. After a few years, ten amendments were added. These amendments are called the Bill of Rights.

James Madison is known as the father of the Constitution. He also helped to write the Bill of Rights.

Continent

see also: Earth, Ocean

A continent is a very large area of land. There are seven continents in the world. People who study continents are called geologists. They study what makes the continents and how continents are formed.

On the move

Continents have not always been where they are now. Millions of years ago there was just one big piece of land. This land split. The continents moved apart. The continents are still moving. They move less than one inch each year.

HOW MUCH LAND?

ASIA	17 million sq. miles
AFRICA	12 million sq. miles
NORTH AMERICA	9 million sq. miles
SOUTH AMERICA	7 million sq. miles
ANTARCTICA	5 million sq. miles
EUROPE	4 million sq. miles
AUSTRALIA	3 million sq. miles

HOW MANY PEOPLE?

ASIA	3.7 billion
AFRICA	807 million
EUROPE	730 million
NORTH AMERICA	481 million
SOUTH AMERICA	349 million
AUSTRALIA	31 million
ANTARCTICA	no permanent residents

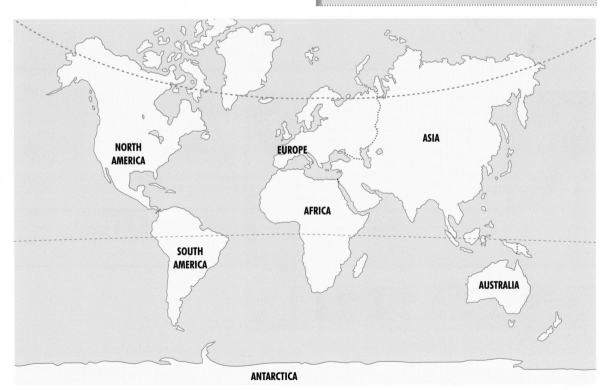

the seven continents

Coral

see also: Coast, Island

Coral is made of the skeletons of tiny animals. Coral has millions of these tiny animals. They are called polyps. Coral forms in shallow, warm seas. Coral can make whole islands. Some large coral areas are called reefs.

Coral reefs

Living polyps form coral reefs. Living polyps attach to the coral that is already there. Some polyps hatch from eggs. Eggs are produced by adult polyps. Other polyps form as buds. The buds form on other polyps. Each new polyp settles on the reef. It makes its own stony skeleton. The skeleton protects it. New polyps build on top of dead polyps. The coral reef grows larger.

CORAL FACTS

NUMBER OF KINDS	2,300
COLOR	orange, yellow, brown, purple, green
LENGTH OF A SINGLE POLYP	1 to 12 inches
LENGTH OF A CORAL REEF	up to 1,250 miles
STATUS	common
LIFE SPAN OF REEF	millions of years
ENEMIES	sea animals, people

This stony coral polyp larva hasn't yet built a stony skeleton around itself.

This coral is part of the Great Barrier Reef in Australia. Some corals look like trees. Other corals look like fans or pipes.

MEAT EATER

A coral polyp feeds at night. It eats floating larvae. Food drifts into its grasp. Its stinging tentacles trap the food. Tiny plants live inside each polyp. The tiny plants make food that the polyp eats.

Costa Rica

see also: North America

Costa Rica is a small country. It is in Central America. It has two coasts. The east coast is hot and wet. The west coast is cooler and drier.

Living in Costa Rica

Costa Rica has beautiful forests. Some Costa Ricans work with tourists who come to see the forests. Some people live in towns. Many people have small farms. Some farmers use brightly-painted ox carts. Farmers grow beans, coffee, and corn. Costa Ricans eat beans and fried or boiled plantains. Plantains are like bananas.

Friends meet in cafés. They sing and play the guitar. People dance to calypso and reggae music.

Bananas from Costa Rica are sold all over the world.

DID YOU KNOW?

Two Costa Rican volcanoes, Mount Poás and Mount Irazu, rumble and steam. No one knows when the volcanoes will erupt.

North America

FACT FILE

PEOPLE	Costa Ricans
POPULATION	almost 4 million
MAIN LANGUAGES	Spanish
CAPITAL CITY	San José
MONEY	Colón
HIGHEST MOUNTAIN	Chirripó-Grande—12,530 feet
LONGEST RIVER	Chirripo – 75 miles

Coyote

see also: Dog, Mammal, Wolf

The coyote is a mammal. It is a kind of wild dog. The coyote lives in the open grassland areas of North America. It is also called prairie wolf and brush wolf.

Coyote families

A male coyote is called a dog. A female coyote is called a bitch. The babies are called pups. About six pups are born at a time. Coyotes live in small family groups called packs. The pups are born in a cave or burrow called a den. Both parents feed and take care of the pups.

COYOTE FACTS

NUMBER OF KINDS	1
COLOR	gray and beige
LENGTH	30 to 40 inches, without tail
HEIGHT	18 to 22 inches
WEIGHT	up to 44 lbs.
STATUS	common
LIFE SPAN	about 4 years
ENEMIES	people

thick fur to keep warm in cold winters

a coyote

a high, loud howl can be heard by other coyotes

sharp teeth for ripping meat

claws for digging

These are four-week-old cubs. They spend a lot of time in their den.

MEAT EATER

Coyotes hunt at night. They hunt for rabbits, ground squirrels, and other small rodents. A small group of coyotes can kill a deer.

Crab

see also: Crustacean, Invertebrate, Sea Life

A crab is a crustacean. It has a hard shell and strong pincers. Most crabs live in sea water. They often live close to shore. Some crabs live in fresh water. Others live on land.

Crab families

A young crab is called a larva. The larva hatches from an egg. The young larva sheds its shell many times as it grows bigger. Some crabs live in burrows. They dig the burrows in the sand. Some crabs hide in cracks in the rocks.

CRAB FACTS

NUMBER OF KINDS....	4,500
COLOR......	brown to red or yellow
LENGTH......	less than one inch to 6 feet
WEIGHT.....	up to 20 lbs.
STATUS.......	common
LIFE SPAN....	up to 12 years
ENEMIES.....	squid, seabirds, people

strong claws with pincers to crush food and attack enemies

a land crab

five pairs of legs called claws

hard shell to protect the body and legs

flat back legs for paddling through water

This female shore crab lays many eggs at a time.

MEAT EATER

Many shore crabs hunt from their burrows. The crab waits for a young turtle or lobster to pass by. The crab grabs it and pulls it into its burrow. Then the crab eats it. Crabs also hunt for worms and small fish.

Crane

see also: Bird

A crane is a large bird. It has a long neck and a long bill. It has long legs and long wings. Cranes live on all continents except Antarctica and South America. Cranes live in marshes. They migrate in the winter to warmer places.

Crane families

Male and female cranes look alike. They dance together. Then they build a nest. The nest is usually built in marshy ground.

The female lays two eggs. Both parents take turns sitting on the eggs until the eggs hatch. The chicks leave the nest as soon as they hatch. The family joins other cranes when the chicks are strong. They form a group called a flock.

This female Florida sandhill crane is waiting for her second egg to hatch.

CRANE FACTS

NUMBER OF KINDS	14
COLOR	mostly gray, black, and white
HEIGHT	up to 5 feet
WEIGHT	up to 17 lbs.
STATUS	some types are endangered
LIFE SPAN	around 20 years
ENEMIES	People drain marshes for farmland, so cranes have fewer places to breed and find food.

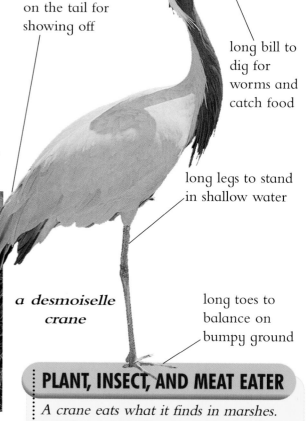

feathers on the head and plumes on the tail for showing off

long bill to dig for worms and catch food

long legs to stand in shallow water

a desmoiselle crane

long toes to balance on bumpy ground

PLANT, INSECT, AND MEAT EATER

A crane eats what it finds in marshes. It eats water plants, worms, and insects. It also eats amphibians and small rodents.

Croatia

see also: Europe, Serbia and Montenegro

Croatia is in southeast Europe. There are hills and mountains. The west coast has hot summers. It has cool, wet winters. Away from the coast, the winter is colder.

Living in Croatia

Half of all Croatians live in old cities and towns. Half of the people live in the country. People eat different foods in different parts of the country. People near the coast eat *brodet*. It is fish cooked with olive oil. It is served with rice, vegetables, and mushrooms. People away from the coast eat stew. The stew is made of beans and fresh corn.

Some Croatians work in factories. Some people work on farms or in mines. Farmers grow grain, cotton, and tobacco. They have fruit and olive trees.

The huge wall in the background used to protect the old town of Dubrovnik.

DID YOU KNOW?

Dubrovnik is an old, walled town. It is on Croatia's Mediterranean coast. It once was an important shipping port. Now many tourists visit Dubrovnik.

Europe

FACT FILE

PEOPLE	Croatians, Croats
POPULATION	about 4.5 million
MAIN LANGUAGE	Croatian
CAPITAL CITY	Zagreb
MONEY	Kuna
HIGHEST MOUNTAIN	Mount Troglav—6,276 feet
LONGEST RIVER	Sava River—584 miles

Crocodile

see also: Alligator, Reptile

The crocodile is a big reptile. It lives in the rivers and lakes of warm places. The crocodile is found in India, Africa, North America, and Australia.

The crocodile is a relative of the alligator. The crocodile's snout is pointed. Its teeth can be seen when its jaws are closed. A crocodile can attack animals, fish, and people.

CROCODILE FACTS

NUMBER OF KINDS...	12
COLOR	greenish-brown
LENGTH	up to 18 feet
WEIGHT....	up to 1,500 lbs.
STATUS	American crocodile is endangered
LIFE SPAN ..	up to 100 years
ENEMIES....	Birds and lizards eat crocodile eggs. People kill crocodiles for their skin.

an American crocodile

thick skin for protection

eyes on top of the head to see while hiding in the water

nostrils that close when underwater

strong tail to swim through water

webbed feet and sharp claws

long teeth to hold fish or animals in the water

A hatchling uses the bump on the end of its snout to poke a hole in the egg's thick skin.

Crocodile families

Babies are called hatchlings. The female digs a nest in the sandy shore. She lays about 60 eggs. The eggs hatch three months later. Then the female gently carries her babies in her mouth. She carries them to the lake or river.

MEAT EATER

Crocodiles eat almost any animal. A big crocodile only needs to eat one or two large animals each year.

Crop

see also: Farming

Crops are farming products. Crops can be food. Crops can be things people use. Some farmers grow crops for just their family. Other farmers grow and sell crops to make money.

Different crops

There are many kinds of crops. Corn, rice, and wheat are grain crops. Fruits and vegetables are also crops. Not all crops are for food. Cotton and flax are crops. They are made into cloth.

Farmers check their crops for pests and diseases. This farmer is checking his cotton field.

DID YOU KNOW?

Corn can be made into fuel for cars and trucks.

Caring for crops

Each kind of crop needs special care. Some crops need extra plant food called fertilizer. Fertilizer helps plants to grow. Other crops need lots of water.

Crops need to be protected from animals, insects, and diseases. Farmers protect crops with fences, scarecrows, and chemical sprays. A fully grown crop is picked, cut down, or dug up. This is called harvesting.

This is a tomato crop. Tomatoes can be grown in large fields.

Crustacean

see also: Animal, Invertebrate, Sea Life

Crustaceans are animals. They have soft bodies. They have hard shells. Crustaceans are invertebrates. Crustaceans shed their shells as they grow bigger. Then they hide until their new, larger shell gets hard.

These freshwater shrimps swim in and out of a crack in a rock.

Crustacean families

All crustaceans lay eggs. Some carry the eggs until they hatch. A shore crab does this. Some do not stay with the eggs. The eggs hatch by themselves.

The eggs hatch as tiny larvae. These are see-through creatures. They have small bristly legs and arms. They eat tiny green plants. They change color as they grow bigger.

Where crustaceans live

Most crustaceans live in water. They are found mostly in the sea. They breathe through gills or through their skin. Some crustaceans live on land. Woodlice live on land in damp wood. Many small crustaceans live on larger animals. These are called parasites. Lice are parasites.

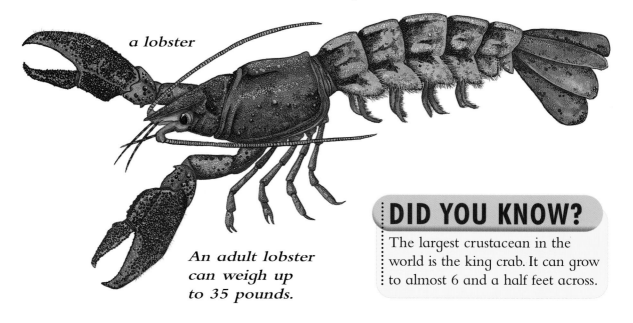

a lobster

An adult lobster can weigh up to 35 pounds.

DID YOU KNOW?

The largest crustacean in the world is the king crab. It can grow to almost 6 and a half feet across.

Cuba

see also: Island, North America

Cuba is an island country. It is in the Caribbean. It is warm and wet. Cuba has beaches and swamps. Hills and forests are in the middle of the island.

Living in Cuba

Many Cubans are farmers. Some have a small amount of land for growing food. They keep pigs and goats. They grow coffee. Sugar cane and tobacco grow on big farms. Houses in the country are usually built of wood. Some houses have palm leaves for roofs. Some have steel roofs.

Cuba was once ruled by Spain. There are old Spanish-style buildings in the towns. The people enjoy music. Guitar players play for customers in cafés. People dance to rumba and salsa music.

Street musicans often play rumba music. Rumba music began in Cuba.

DID YOU KNOW?

Christopher Columbus probably landed in Cuba in 1492. Spanish settlers started moving to Cuba in 1511.

North America

FACT FILE

PEOPLE	Cubans
POPULATION	11 million
MAIN LANGUAGE	Spanish
CAPITAL CITY	Havana
MONEY	Cuban peso
HIGHEST MOUNTAIN	Pico Turquino—6,564 feet
LONGEST RIVER	Cauto River—150 miles

Czech Republic

see also: Europe, Slovakia

The Czech Republic is a country in central Europe. It has mountains and lowlands. The mountains are the wettest areas. Winters are cold. Summers are hot.

Living in the Czech Republic

Most Czechs live in cities and towns. People work in factories, farms, and mines. Farmers grow grain, root crops, flax, and sweet peppers. These peppers are ground up into a spice called paprika.

The people eat cheese that is rolled in bread crumbs and then fried. Meat is often cooked in a creamy sauce.

The Czech people are famous for making things from glass. They make crystal bowls and glasses. The crystal has a pattern cut into the glass.

Prague is an old city. It has old buildings and large public squares. Tourists enjoy visiting Prague.

DID YOU KNOW?

Most of this area used to be called Bohemia. After World War I it was called the Czech Republic.

Europe

FACT FILE

PEOPLE	Czechs
POPULATION	about 10 million
MAIN LANGUAGES	Czech, Slovak
CAPITAL CITY	Prague
MONEY	Koruna
HIGHEST MOUNTAIN	Mount Snezka—5,255 feet
LONGEST RIVER	Labe River—705 miles

Dance

see also: Ballet, Music

Dancing is moving to music or to a rhythm. Some dances have rules that control the steps. Ballet is one dance form that has many rules. Some dances have very few rules. People make their movements fit the music.

Dancing around the world

Most countries have their own dances. Some cultures have dances for important events. They might have special dances for weddings and harvest time. Some religions use dance. It is a part of worship. It can be part of a ceremony.

These dancers have very few dancing rules. They are dancing to pop music.

DID YOU KNOW?

In some cultures, dances are believed to have magical powers. Native Americans have dances to cure people who are ill or to change the weather.

These kathak dancers from India follow strict rules. The rules tell them how to move. The rules tell them what expression they must have on their faces.

Day and Night

see also: Season

Day is when the sun has risen. It is light outside. Night is when the sun has set. It is dark outside. The earth spins around once every 24 hours. Nearly every part of the earth has some hours of light during the day. Nearly every part of the earth has some hours of darkness.

Life at night

People and most animals are active during the day. They sleep during the night. Some people work at night and sleep during the day. Some animals are nocturnal. This means that they hunt for food at night. They sleep during some part of the day. Some birds, such as the owl, hunt at night. They have eyes that can see well in the dark.

Different parts of the earth face the sun at different times of the day. As the earth spins, parts that were light are no longer facing the sun. They become dark. Parts that were dark move into the light as they face the sun.

Some animals, like this aardwolf, look for food at night. They rely on special eyesight, good hearing, or sense of smell to find food.

> **STAY SAFE**
>
> Human beings do not see well in the dark. Always wear reflective or light clothing when walking or riding a bicycle at night. Always use a light on your bicycle after dark.

> **DID YOU KNOW?**
>
> In Canada, winter days are short and the nights are long. At the same time in Australia, it is summer, and the days are long and the nights are short.

Declaration of Independence

see also: American Revolution; Independence Day; Jefferson, Thomas

The Declaration of Independence was written in 1776. It is an important document because it said that Americans wanted to become an independent nation.

The American Revolution

Before 1776, Britain ruled thirteen colonies on the east coast of North America. In 1775, the colonists began to fight the British soldiers. The American Revolution began.

Making the Declaration

A group of leaders from all the colonies met during the Revolution. In 1776, they decided the colonies should unite and form their own government. Thomas Jefferson was chosen to write the Declaration of Independence.

The Declaration of Independence was approved on July 4, 1776. It announced to the world that a new nation had been founded.

DID YOU KNOW?

The original Declaration is in the National Archives in Washington, D.C.

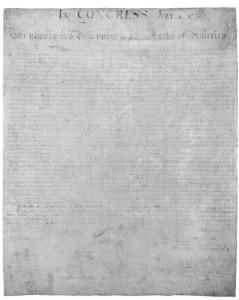

The Declaration of Independence is only one page long.

What does the Declaration say?

The Declaration of Independence says people are equal and have a right to life, liberty, and happiness. It says Americans would start a new kind of government that was fair to everyone.

This painting shows the signing of the Declaration of Independence.

Deer

see also: Antelope, Mammal, Moose

Deer are large mammals. They eat plants. They live in forests, grasslands, swamps, and deserts. They are found in North and South America, Asia, Europe, and North Africa.

Deer families

Male deer are called bucks, stags, or bulls. Female deer are called does, hinds, or cows. The doe usually has one baby at a time. It is called a fawn or calf. Some deer live alone. Most live in a large group called a herd. Deer roam looking for food. Herds of caribou deer walk thousands of miles each year to escape the cold Arctic winter.

DEER FACTS

NUMBER OF KINDS	more than 60
COLOR	brown or tan
HEIGHT	1 to 7 feet
WEIGHT	20 to 1,800 lbs.
STATUS	some types are endangered
LIFE SPAN	10 to 20 years
ENEMIES	bears, wolves, coyotes, cougars, people

antlers for fighting

large ears to listen for danger

hairy coat to keep warm

long, thin legs to run fast

hooves to protect the feet

a whitetail deer

PLANT EATER

Deer usually feed in the early morning or early evening. Deer eat leaves, grass, and bark. Deer swallow their food first. Later they bring a mouthful of food back up from their stomachs. Then they chew it.

The spotted coat of the fawn helps it hide from its enemies.

Delaware

see also: United States of America

Delaware is a state in the eastern United States of America. The state is on the Delmarva peninsula. The land in Delaware is mostly flat. There are hills in the north. In the south is the Great Cypress Swamp, where the land is wet. Many rivers run through the state into Delaware Bay. The weather in Delaware is mild. There is a lot of rain.

A farm worker harvests hay in Odessa, Delaware. Flat land makes farming with modern machinery much easier.

In the past

Settlers from Sweden came to North America in the 1600s. Many of them settled in Delaware when it was a colony. They built the first log cabins in North America.

Life in Delaware

Most people in Delaware live in the north of the state. Much of the rest of the state is covered in farmland. Farmers raise chickens and grow soybeans and corn. Other people in Delaware work in the chemicals industry.

DID YOU KNOW?

The people of Delaware were the first to approve the United States Constitution. This means that Delaware was the first state to join the United States of America.

Delaware

FACT FILE

BECAME A STATE	1787 (1st state)
LAND AREA	1,954 square miles (49th largest land area)
POPULATION	817,491 (45th most populated state)
OTHER NAMES	Diamond State, First State
CAPITAL CITY	Dover

DECEMBER 7, 1787

Delta

see also: Coast, River

A delta is low land. It is where a big river flows into the sea. Three rivers with large deltas are the Nile, the Mississippi, and the Ganges. Not all rivers have deltas.

How are deltas made?

As a river flows, it picks up rock, soil, and mud. The river carries these things along and drops them when it flows into the sea. The rock, soil, and mud form a delta. The river flows through the delta. It divides into many smaller rivers. The smaller rivers divide the land. This makes the land look like the fingers of a hand.

This is the Mississippi delta. The Mississippi River divides into many smaller rivers as it flows into the sea.

People and deltas

The rich delta soil is good for growing crops, so people often live on or near deltas. Sometimes the river floods the delta. Flooding makes the delta a dangerous place to live.

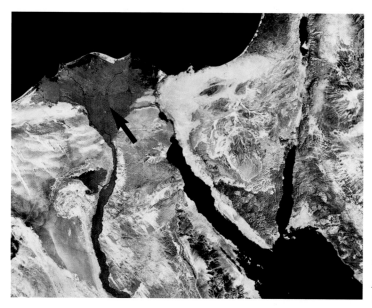

DID YOU KNOW?

The ancient Greek alphabet had a letter called delta. It was written as Δ. This is the same shape as the land where a river flows into the sea. The name of this letter was used to describe the delta-shaped land.

This is the Nile River delta in Egypt. This picture was taken from a satellite.

Democratic Republic of Congo

see also: Africa

The Democratic Republic of Congo (DRC) is the third largest country in Africa. DRC has a very short seacoast along the Atlantic Ocean. Half of the country is lowlands. The lowlands have winding rivers. There are some mountains in the east. Large areas are rain forest. The weather is hot and wet.

Living in the Democratic Republic of Congo

Many people live in the country. Most of them work on farms. They grow rice, cassava, and bananas. Less than half of the people live in towns and cities.

There have been wars in the DRC for many years. This makes it hard for people to find work and to improve their lives.

DID YOU KNOW?

In the Democratic Republic of Congo, there are more than 200 local languages.

One group of people in the DRC is the pygmy tribe. They are smaller than most other people. They have a very old culture.

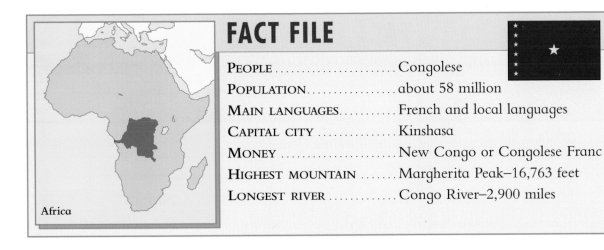

Africa

FACT FILE

PEOPLE	Congolese
POPULATION	about 58 million
MAIN LANGUAGES	French and local languages
CAPITAL CITY	Kinshasa
MONEY	New Congo or Congolese Franc
HIGHEST MOUNTAIN	Margherita Peak—16,763 feet
LONGEST RIVER	Congo River—2,900 miles

Denmark

see also: Europe

Denmark is a country in northwest Europe. It is mainly lowlands. It has many islands. The east central area is hilly. Winters are cool and wet. Summers are warm.

Living in Denmark

Most people live in towns or cities. Many people ride bicycles. There are many bicycle paths.

The main foods are fish, meat, and potatoes. *Frikadeller* is fried pork meatballs, potatoes, and red cabbage. *Gravad lax* is salmon and dill. It is served with mustard sauce.

Farmers grow grain, flax, hemp, hops, and tobacco. Ships, engines, and furniture are made in Denmark. Building materials such as limestone, clay, and gravel come from the ground.

The Little Mermaid is the main character in one of Hans Christian Andersen's fairy tales. This statue of her is in Copenhagen Harbor.

DID YOU KNOW?

Hans Christian Andersen wrote many fairy tales. He was born in Denmark.

Europe

FACT FILE

PEOPLE	Danes, Danish
POPULATION	about 5 million
MAIN LANGUAGE	Danish
CAPITAL CITY	Copenhagen
MONEY	Krone
HIGHEST MOUNTAIN	Yding Skovhøj—568 feet
LONGEST RIVER	Guden River—98 miles

Desert

see also: Cactus, Camel, Climate

A desert is a place that is very dry. It can be hot or cold during the day. Most deserts are always cold at night. Deserts are in all the continents except Europe. Most deserts are bare rock or sand.

Desert life

Cactus plants live in hot deserts. They store water in their stems. Wild grass and flowers grow quickly in deserts. They grow after it rains. An oasis is a place in the desert where there is water. Plants and trees grow near this water.

Animals live in hot deserts. Snakes, scorpions, rats, and camels live there. Some animals live underground during the hot days. They come out during the cool nights.

Oil is found under some deserts, such as the Arabian Desert.

DID YOU KNOW?

The driest place on earth is the Atacama Desert. It is in Chile.

The Sahara Desert is in northern Africa. It is the largest desert in the world. The name Sahara comes from the Arabic word for desert.

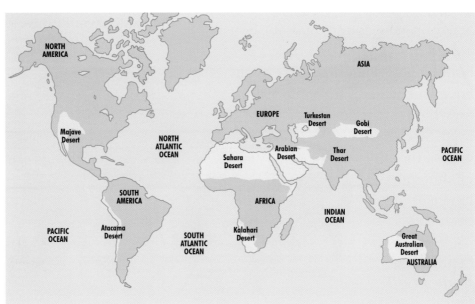

These are the biggest deserts of the world.

Dinosaur

see also: Brachiosaurus, Fossil

Dinosaurs are animals that lived millions of years ago. The word dinosaur means "terrible lizard." There were many kinds of dinosaurs. Some dinosaurs, such as Brachiosaurus, were bigger than a house. Some dinosaurs were so small that they were the size of a chicken.

These scientists are looking for dinosaur bones.

The age of the dinosaurs

Dinosaurs lived on Earth for 150 million years. They roamed everywhere. Some dinosaurs were meat eaters. Tyrannosaurus was a meat eater. Other dinosaurs ate only plants. Brachiosaurus was a plant eater.

How we know about dinosaurs

Scientists have found dinosaur bones buried in soil, sand, and rock. The bones tell us what dinosaurs might have looked like. The bones tell us how they might have lived. Scientists believe that all dinosaurs hatched from eggs.

Dinosaurs came in all shapes and sizes.

What happened?

No one knows for sure why the dinosaurs died out about 65 million years ago. Some scientists think that the climate and temperature changed. Dinosaurs couldn't change, so they died out. Other scientists think a comet might have hit the earth causing storms and winds. Dust might have blocked the sunlight. Many animals, including dinosaurs, would have died.

Dog

see also: Coyote, Mammal, Wolf

A dog is a mammal. Some dogs
are trained to work. Most dogs
are kept as pets. Dingoes,
wolves, coyotes, and jackals are
members of the dog family.
They are wild dogs.

Dog families

A male dog is called a dog. A female
dog is called a bitch. Young dogs are
called puppies. The female has from
three to ten puppies at a time.
A puppy is ready to go to a
new home when it is about
ten weeks old. Wild dogs live
in groups called packs. Wild
dogs care for their puppies
in a den.

DOG FACTS

NUMBER OF KINDS	more than 330
COLOR	brown, black, white, blond, or a mixture of these
HEIGHT	5 to 34 inches
WEIGHT	3 to 210 lbs.
STATUS	common
LIFE SPAN	usually 10 to 12 years
ENEMIES	other dogs, people

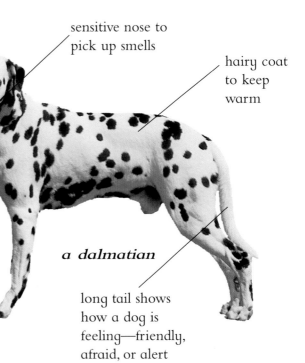

sensitive nose to
pick up smells

hairy coat
to keep
warm

long tongue
to lap up
water

a dalmatian

long tail shows
how a dog is
feeling—friendly,
afraid, or alert

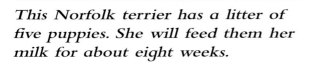

**This Norfolk terrier has a litter of
five puppies. She will feed them her
milk for about eight weeks.**

PLANT, INSECT, AND MEAT EATER

*A dog eats almost anything. It likes
meat. Wild dogs hunt in packs. They
chase antelope.*

Dolphin

see also: Mammal, Sea Life, Whale

A dolphin is a mammal. Dolphins live in all but the coldest oceans and seas. Two well-known types of dolphins are the common dolphin and the bottle-nosed dolphin.

air hole for breathing

beak with teeth to hold slippery fish

DOLPHIN FACTS

NUMBER OF KINDS... 36
COLOR ..... gray
LENGTH .... 5 to 13 ft.
WEIGHT.... 150 to 550 lbs.
STATUS ..... common
LIFE SPAN .. 25 to 50 years
ENEMIES.... Few people hunt dolphins, but thousands are trapped each year in fishing nets.

dorsal fin to swim straight

MEAT EATER

Schools of dolphins chase fish to eat them. Dolphins find their food by using sound waves. This is called echolocation.

a bottle-nosed dolphin

strong tail fins to swim fast

A mother bottle-nosed dolphin and her calf swim along the sea bottom.

Dolphin families

A female dolphin gives birth to one baby at a time. The baby is called a calf. A calf can swim as soon as it is born. It stays close to its mother or another female for about one year. Dolphins travel around the sea in groups called schools.

Dominican Republic

see also: Island, North America

The Dominican Republic is a country on the island of Hispaniola. It is in the Caribbean Sea. The land has mountains with forests. It has flat plains. It is mostly hot and wet. It is cooler high in the mountains.

Living in the Dominican Republic

More than half of Dominicans live in towns. Many people work with tourists who visit the Dominican Republic. Large farms in the country grow sugar cane. Factories turn the sugar cane into a sweet brown syrup called molasses.

Every year there is a carnival. It is on Shrove Tuesday. There are displays and parades. Dominicans dance the merengue.

There are many Spanish-style buildings in the Dominican Republic.

DID YOU KNOW?

Dominicans say that the explorer Christopher Columbus is buried in the old cathedral of Santo Domingo.

FACT FILE

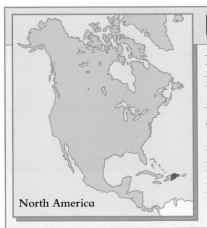

North America

PEOPLE	Dominicans
POPULATION	almost 9 million
MAIN LANGUAGE	Spanish
CAPITAL CITY	Santo Domingo
MONEY	Peso
HIGHEST MOUNTAIN	Pico Duarte—10,420 feet
LONGEST RIVER	Yaque del Norte—74 miles

Dragonfly

see also: Insect

An adult dragonfly is a large insect with shiny wings. It spends most of its life as a nymph with a thick body and no wings. The nymph lives in ponds, lakes, or rivers. The nymph leaves the water to become an adult dragonfly with four wings.

DRAGONFLY FACTS

NUMBER OF KINDS	5,000
COLOR	blue, red, or green with black, white, or yellow patterns
WINGSPAN	up to 6 inches
STATUS	common
LIFE SPAN	up to 5 years
ENEMIES	birds, spiders, other insects, crocodiles

large eyes to see very small movements

six spiky legs to catch insects as it flies

MEAT AND INSECT EATER

A dragonfly can eat as it flies. It makes a basket with its legs. It catches small flying insects in the basket. Then it holds the insect in its legs or mouth.

four large wings to fly faster than most birds

a dragonfly

long, thin body to steer itself through the air

Dragonfly families

A young dragonfly is called a nymph. It hatches from an egg laid in water. It eats insects, tadpoles, and small fish. It might be a nymph from one to five years. Then it changes into an adult dragonfly. It lives only for a few weeks or months as an adult.

This adult dragonfly is just coming out of its nymph stage.

Drama

see also: Literature

Drama is acting out a story or an idea. It is performed in front of an audience. Plays, films, and TV programs tell dramatic stories. Drama probably began thousands of years ago. People began by miming. Then they added words to dances.

> **DID YOU KNOW?**
> A comedy is funny and has a happy ending. A tragedy is sad or serious and usually has a sad ending.

How drama changed

Drama as it is today began 2,000 years ago. It began in Greece and Egypt. People began using scenery. They used costumes and makeup. These things helped the audience understand the story. Today many people enjoy drama. They enjoy theater performances. They watch films, videos, and TV. They listen to radio drama.

This scene is from a Greek tragedy. The actors are wearing masks instead of makeup.

This scene is from a movie of Shakespeare's play Romeo and Juliet. *This play has been made into a movie many times.*

> **WILLIAM SHAKESPEARE (1564–1616)**
> Shakespeare wrote 40 plays. Some of them are very famous plays. His plays include *Hamlet* and *Julius Caesar.* People perform, read, and study his plays.

Drug

A drug is a chemical. Medicines are made up of drugs. Medicines can cure diseases and make people and animals feel better.

People and drugs

People have used drugs for thousands of years. Many plants have natural drugs. A long time ago wise people knew which plants to give to sick people. Most drugs are made in factories. Some drugs can be bought in stores, such as cough syrup and aspirin. Some drugs can only be bought with a note from a doctor. The note is called a prescription.

Drugs can be taken in many ways. Creams are rubbed on the skin. Pills and syrups are swallowed. Injections put drugs into the blood. Gases and sprays are breathed in.

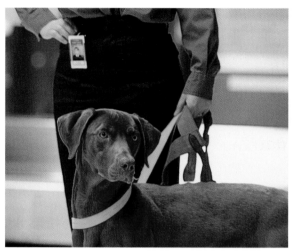

Trained "sniffer" dogs sniff out hidden, illegal drugs. They work at airports and shipping ports.

STAY SAFE

Children should never take any medicines by themselves. Medicines should only be given to them by an adult they trust.

Addictive and illegal drugs

Some drugs are addictive. This means that the person who takes this drug wants more and more of it. It is very hard for an addict to stop wanting the drug. Nicotine in cigarettes and alcohol in drinks can be addictive. Illegal drugs are not allowed by law. They are dangerous drugs. Heroin and cocaine are both addictive and illegal drugs.

These pills are made in a factory. They are made to help sick people get better.